AUDIO ACCESS INCLUDED 🔊 Recorded Accompaniments Online

SONGS FROM

21ST CENTURY MOVIE MUSICALS FOR WOMEN SINGERS

To access recorded accompaniments online, visit:
www.halleonard.com/mylibrary

Enter Code
5871-7741-6518-7749

ISBN 978-1-5400-2610-1

Visit Hal Leonard Online at
www.halleonard.com

Contact Us:
Hal Leonard
7777 West Bluemound Road
Milwaukee, WI 53213
Email: info@halleonard.com

In Europe contact:
Hal Leonard Europe Limited
Distribution Centre, Newmarket Road
Bury St Edmunds, Suffolk, IP33 3YB
Email: info@halleonardeurope.com

In Australia contact:
Hal Leonard Australia Pty. Ltd.
4 Lentara Court
Cheltenham, Victoria, 3192 Australia
Email: info@halleonard.com.au

All piano accompaniments performed by Brendan Fox except *Still Hurting*, performed by Jason Robert Brown.

IF ONLY
from the Disney Channel Original Movie *Descendants*

Words and Music by Adam Anders,
Nikki Hassman and Par Astrom

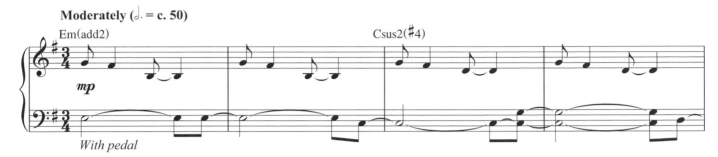

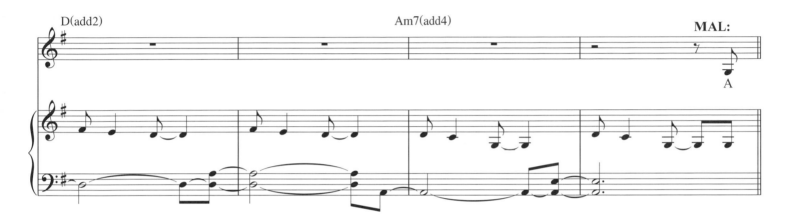

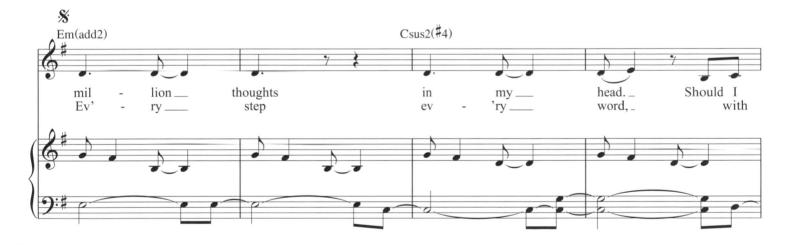

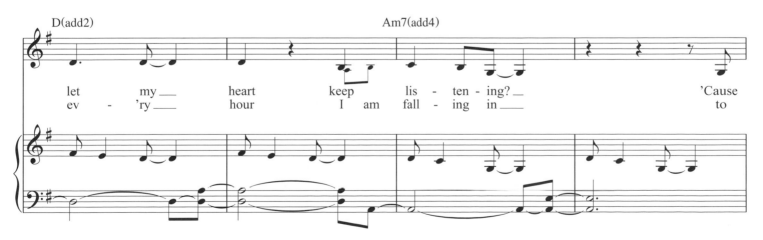

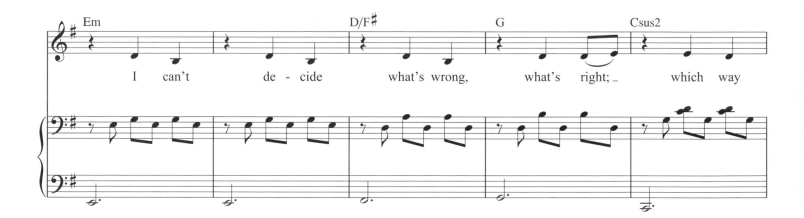

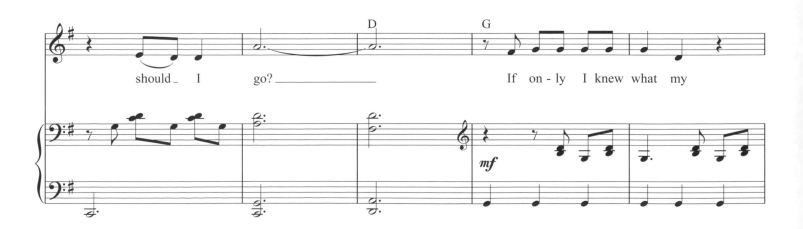

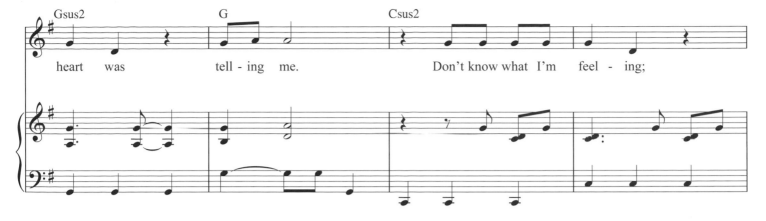

heart was tell - ing me. Don't know what I'm feel - ing;

is this ___ just a ___ dream? ___ Ah oh, _____

yeah. If on - ly I could read the signs in ___ front of me,

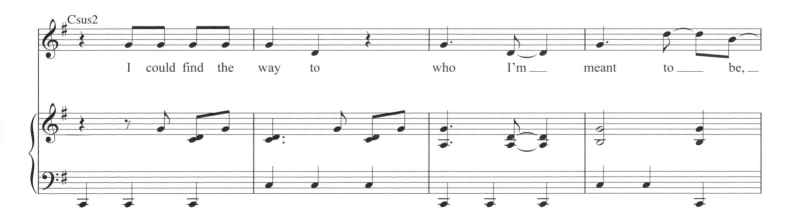

I could find the way to who I'm ___ meant to ___ be, ___

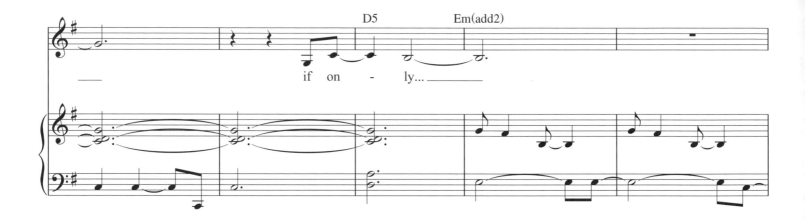

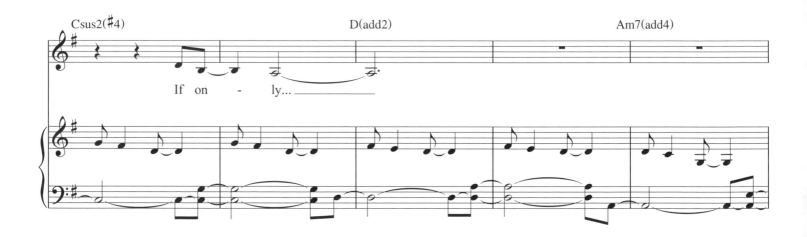

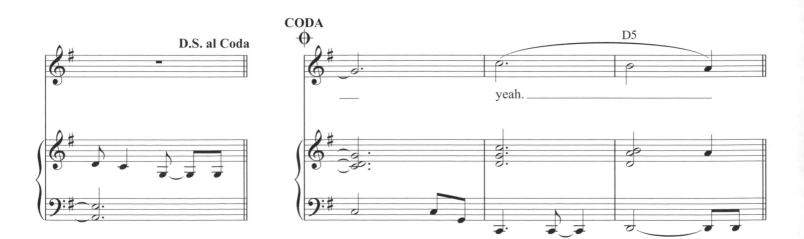

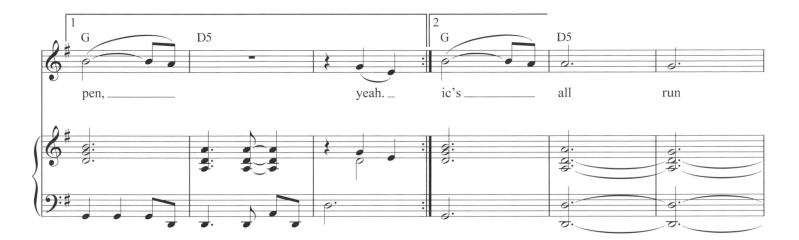

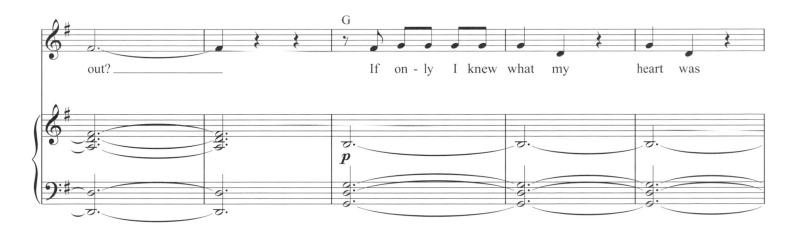

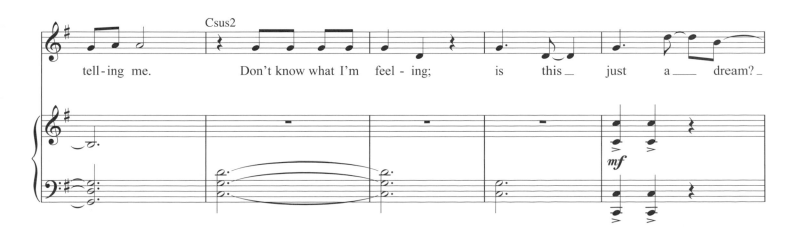

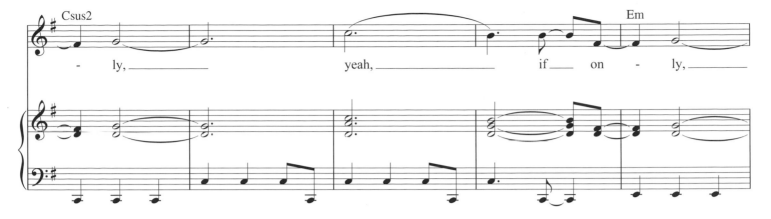

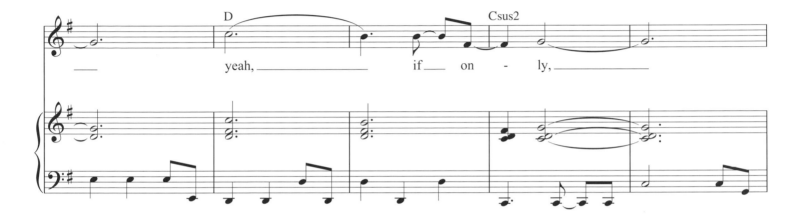

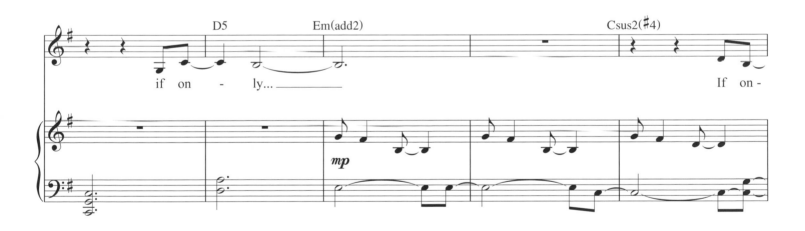

TRUE LOVE'S KISS
from *Enchanted*

Music by Alan Menken
Lyrics by Stephen Schwartz

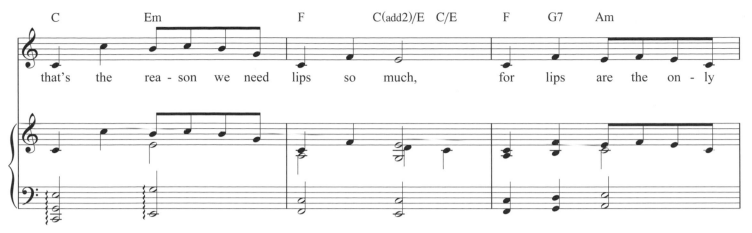

that's the rea-son we need lips so much, for lips are the on-ly

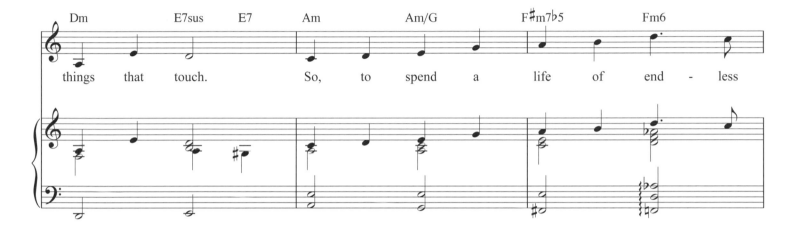

things that touch. So, to spend a life of end-less

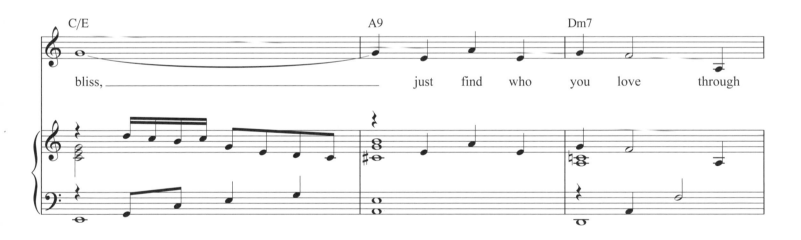

bliss,_____ just find who you love through

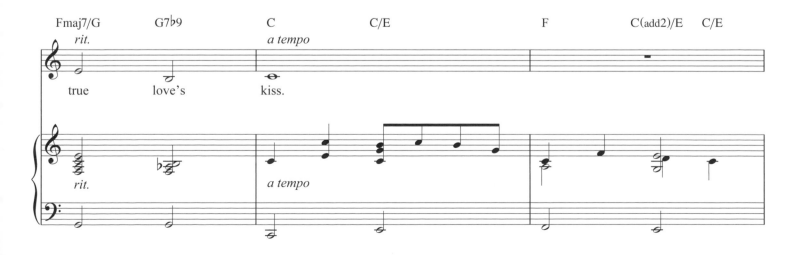

true love's kiss.

12

13

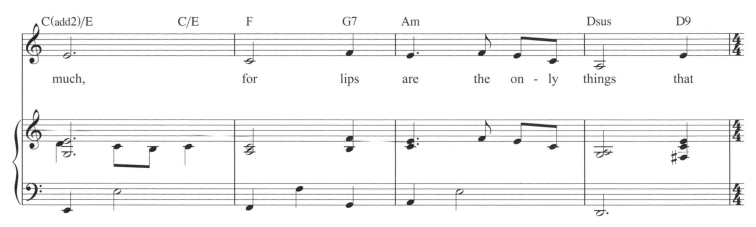

much, for lips are the on-ly things that

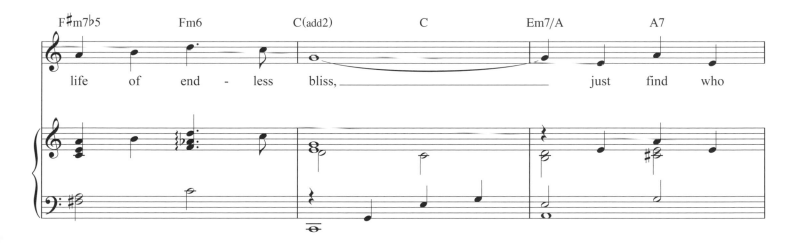

touch. So, to spend a

life of end-less bliss, _____ just find who

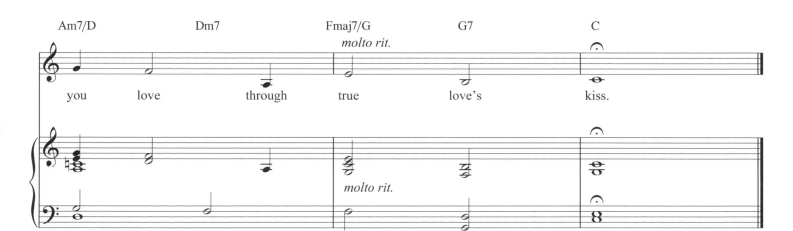

you love through true love's kiss.

FOR THE FIRST TIME IN FOREVER

from *Frozen*

Music and Lyrics by Kristen Anderson-Lopez
and Robert Lopez

With excitement

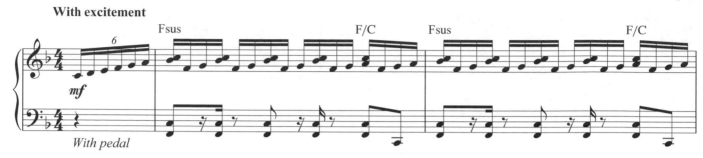

The win-dow is o - pen! So's _ that door! _ I

did-n't know they did that an - y - more. _ Who knew we owned _ eight thou - sand sal - ad

plates? For years I've roamed _ these emp - ty halls. _

Why have a ball - room with no balls? Fi - nal - ly, they're o - p'ning up the

gates! There'll be ac - tual real live peo - ple;

it - 'll be to - tal - ly, strange. But, wow! am I so read - y for this

Expressively

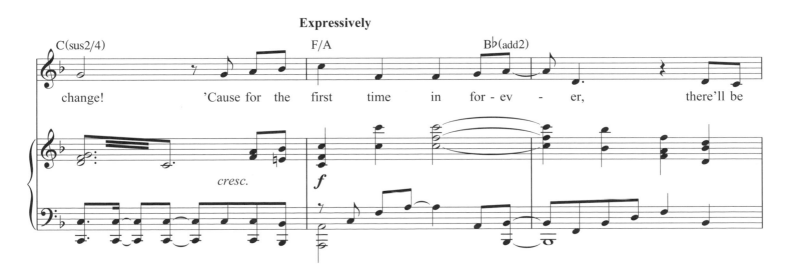

change! 'Cause for the first time in for - ev - er, there'll be

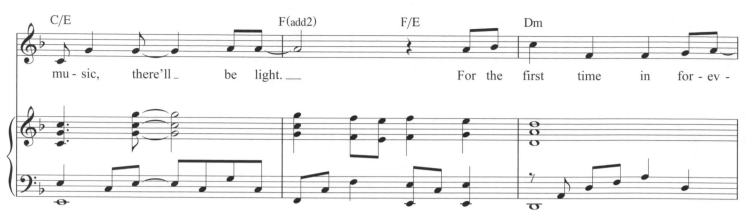

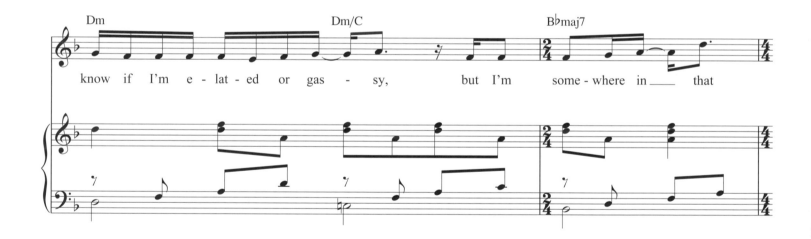

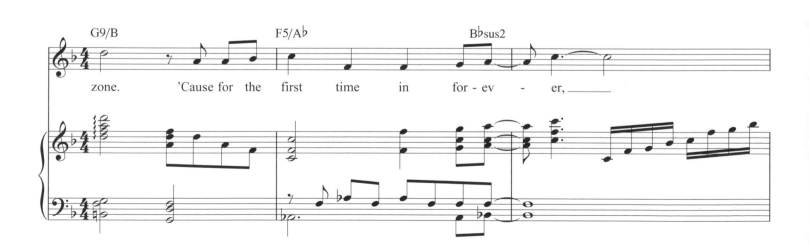

Excited again

I won't be — a - lone. — *(Spoken:) I can't wait to meet everyone. (gasp) What if I meet...*

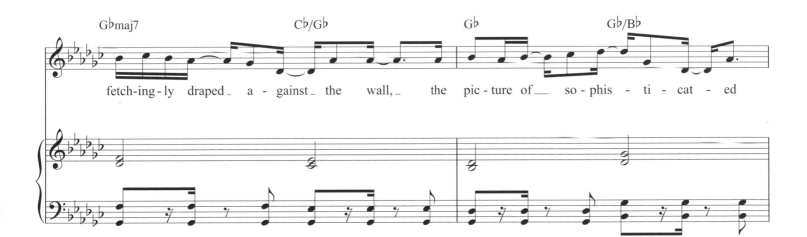

THE one? *(Sung:)* To - night, i - mag - ine me, gown — and all, —

fetch - ing - ly draped — a - gainst — the wall, — the pic - ture of — so - phis - ti - cat - ed

grace. I sud - den - ly see — him stand - ing there: — a

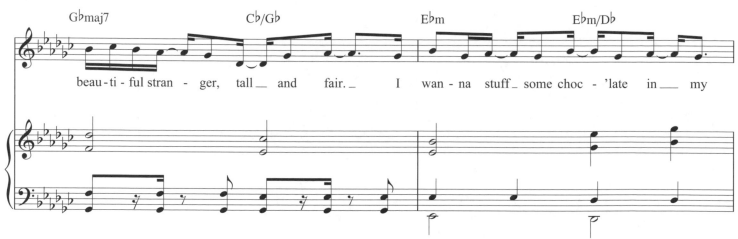

beau-ti-ful stran - ger, tall — and fair. — I wan-na stuff — some choc - 'late in — my

face! But then we laugh and talk — all eve - ning, which is

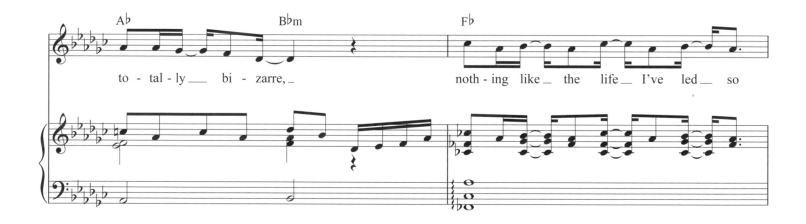

to - tal-ly — bi - zarre, — noth-ing like — the life — I've led — so

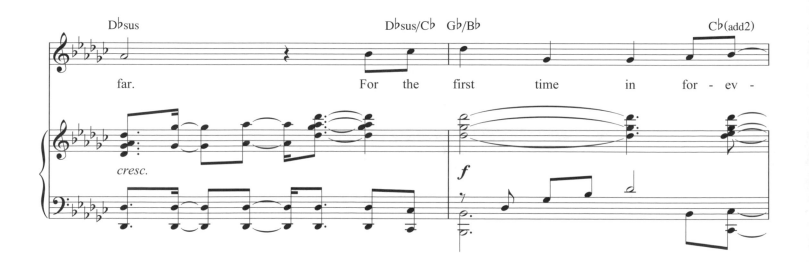

far. For the first time in for - ev -

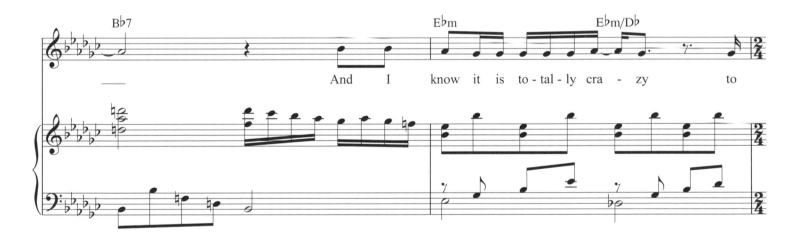

at least_ I've got_ a chance._

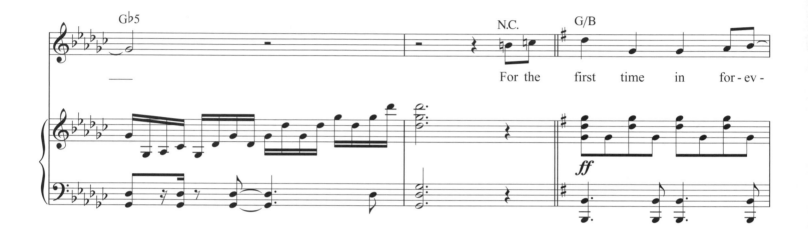

_____ For the first time in for-ev-

-er, I'm get-ting what I'm dream-ing of: _____ a

chance to change_ my lone-ly world, a chance to find_ true love._

I know it all ends to-mor-row, ___ so it

has to be ___ to - day. 'Cause for the first time in for-ev-

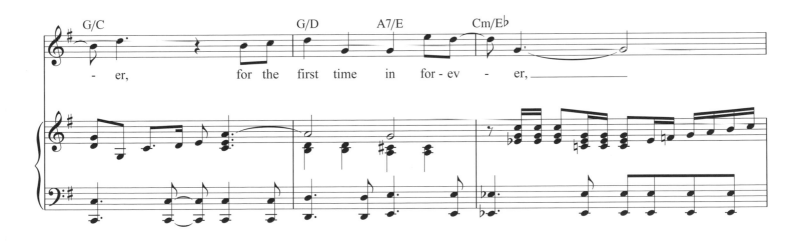

- er, for the first time in for-ev - er, _____

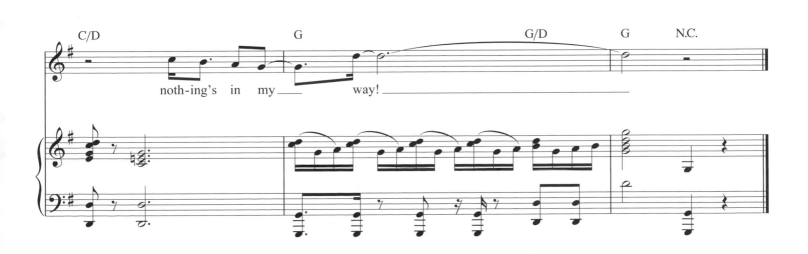

noth-ing's in my ___ way! _____

LET IT GO
from *Frozen*

Music and Lyrics by Kristen Anderson-Lopez
and Robert Lopez

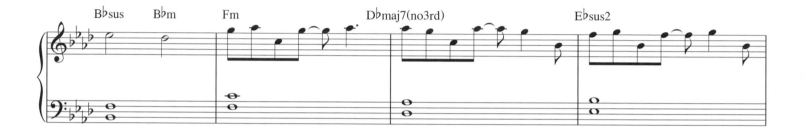

-tion, and it looks like I'm the queen.

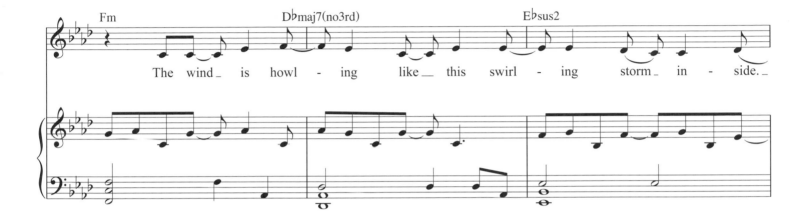

The wind is howl - ing like this swirl - ing storm in - side.

Could-n't keep it in, heav - en knows I

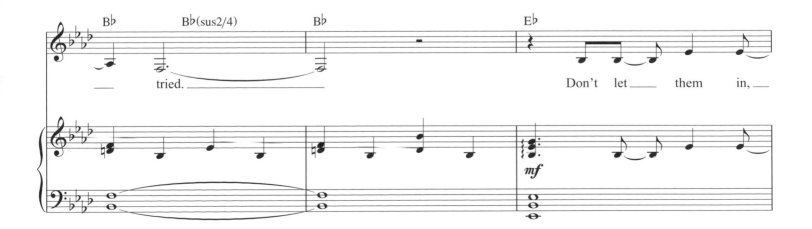

tried. Don't let them in,

24

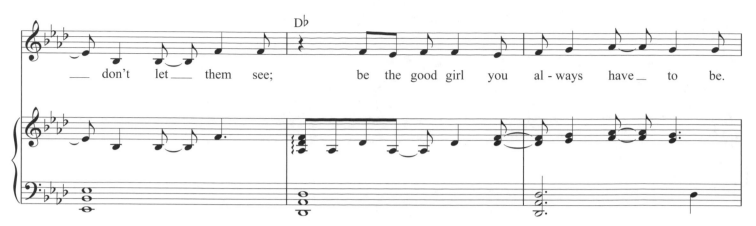

don't let them see; be the good girl you al-ways have to be.

Con-ceal, don't feel, don't let them know...

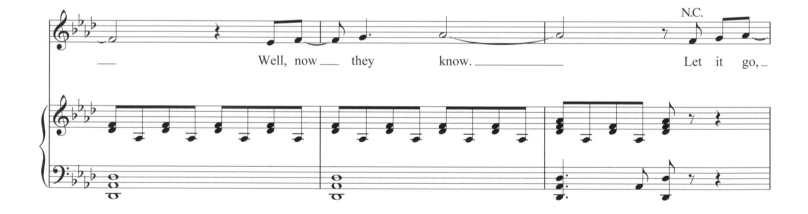

Well, now they know. Let it go,

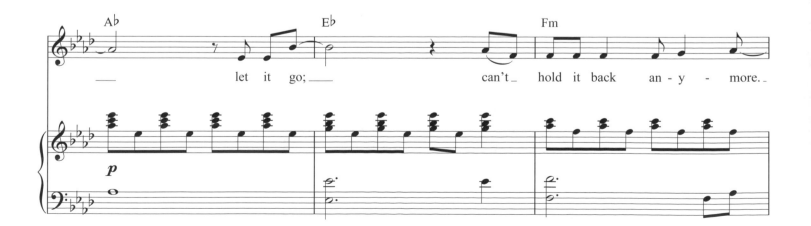

let it go; can't hold it back an-y-more.

Let it go, ____ let it go; ____ turn a - way ____

____ and slam ____ the ___ door. _ I _____ don't _ care ____

____ what they're going to ___ say; _____ let the

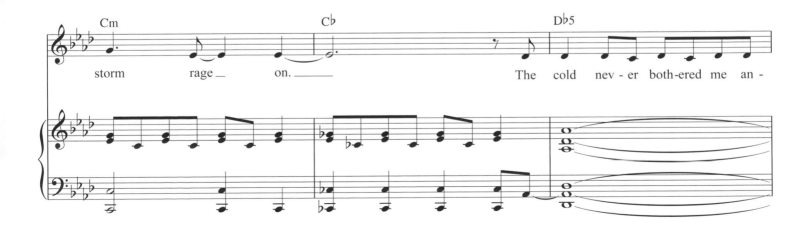

storm rage __ on. _____ The cold nev - er both-ered me an -

Gaining confidence

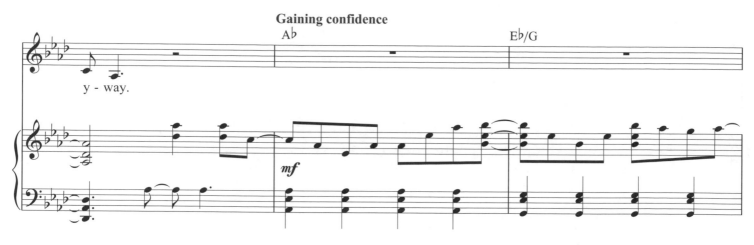

y - way.

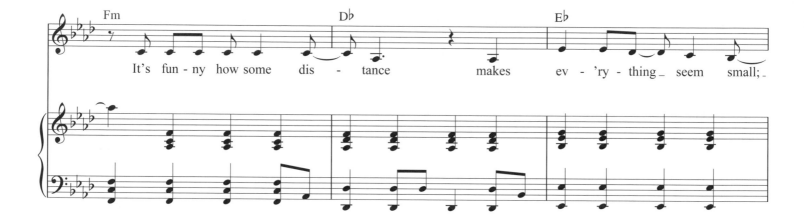

It's fun - ny how some dis - tance makes ev - 'ry - thing _ seem small; _

_ and the fears that once _ con - trolled _ me can't

get to me _ at all. _ It's time _ to see _

27

what I ___ can do, to test ___ the lim - its and ___ break through.

___ No right, ___ no wrong, ___ no rules ___ for me, _____ I'm

free! _____ Let it go, ___ let it go; _

___ I am one ___ with the wind ___ and sky. _____ Let it go, _

let it go; ___ you'll nev - er see ___ me ___

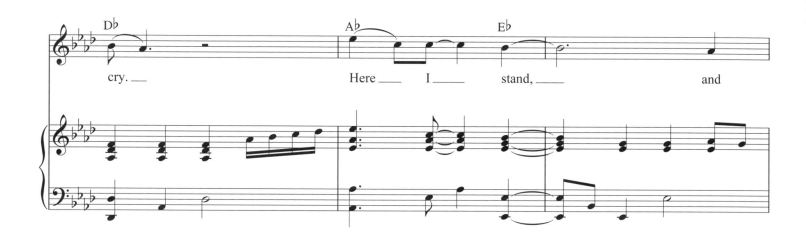

cry. ___ Here ___ I ___ stand, ___ and

here I'll ___ stay; ___ let the storm rage ___ on. ___

My pow - er flur - ries through _ the air _

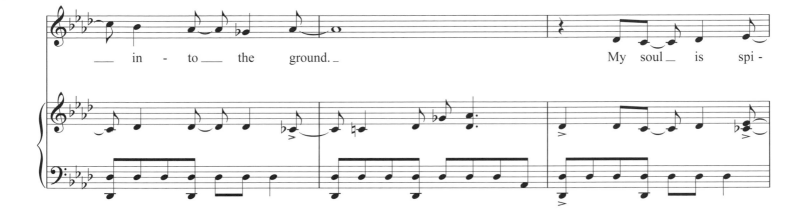

_ in - to _ the ground. _ My soul _ is spi -

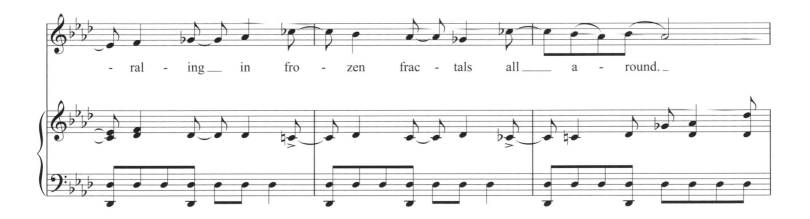

-ral - ing _ in fro - zen frac - tals all _ a - round. _

And one _ thought cry - stal - li - zes like _ an i - cy blast: _

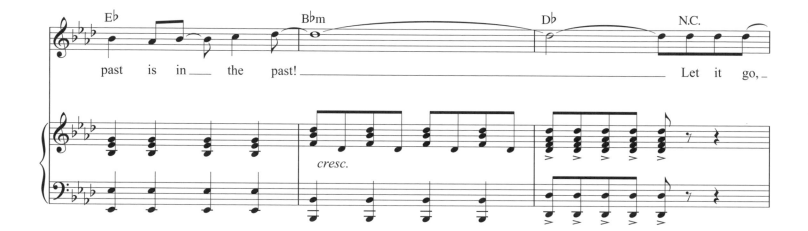

-fect girl ___ is ___ gone. ___ Here ___ I ___ stand ___

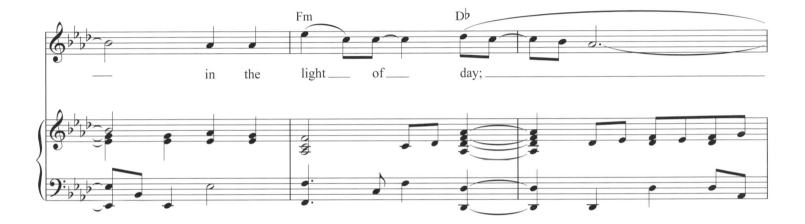

___ in the light ___ of ___ day; ___

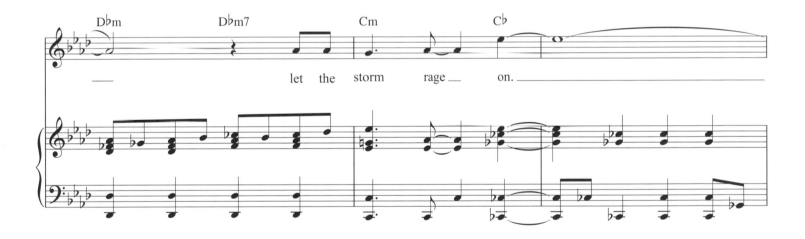

___ let the storm rage ___ on. ___

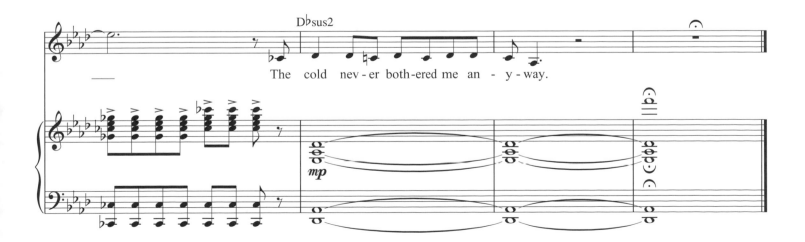

The cold nev-er both-ered me an-y-way.

NEVER ENOUGH
from *The Greatest Showman*

Words and Music by Benj Pasek
and Justin Paul

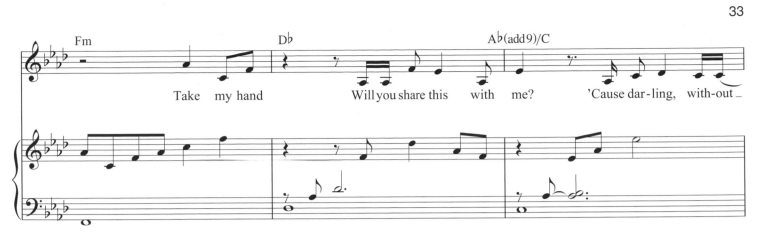

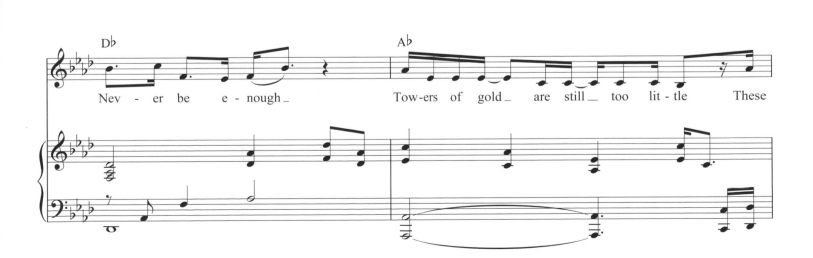

hands couldhold theworld, but it-'ll nev-er be e-nough __ Nev-er be e-

nough _____ for me ___ Nev-er, nev-er

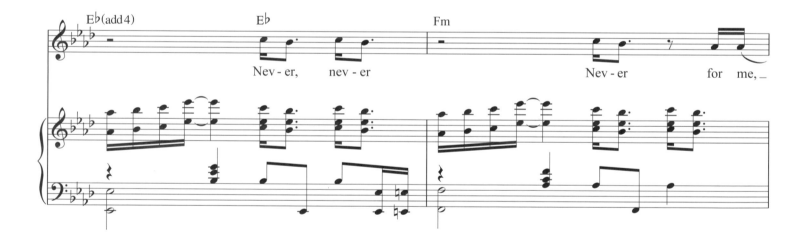

Nev-er, nev-er Nev-er for me,__

__ for me __ Nev-er e-nough_

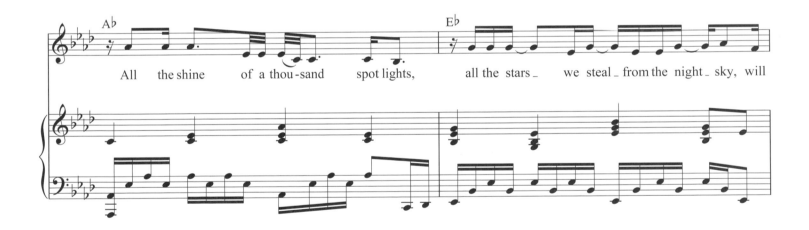

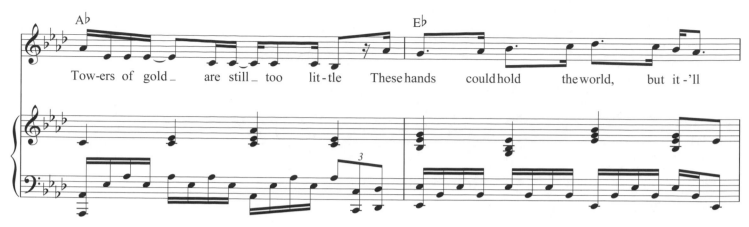

Tow-ers of gold _ are still _ too lit-tle These hands could hold the world, but it -'ll

nev - er be e - nough _ Nev - er be e - nough _____

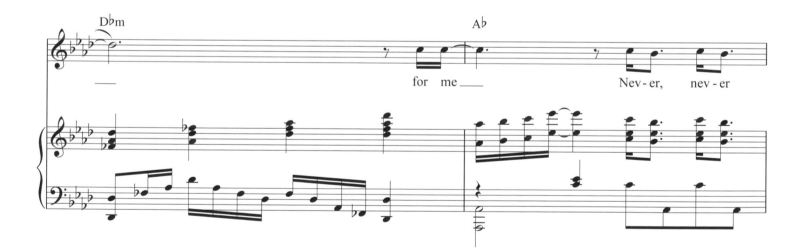

_____ for me _____ Nev - er, nev - er

Nev - er, nev - er Nev - er, for me, _

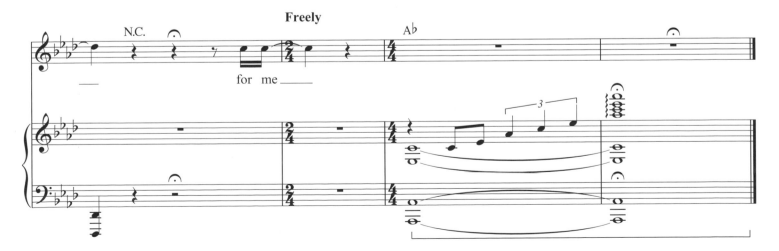

TIGHTROPE
from *The Greatest Showman*

Words and Music by Benj Pasek
and Justin Paul

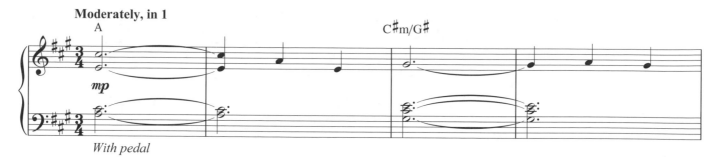

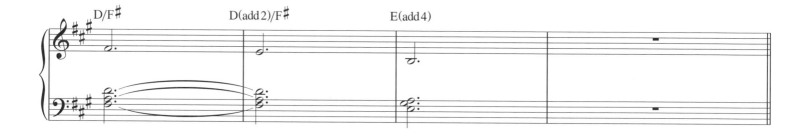

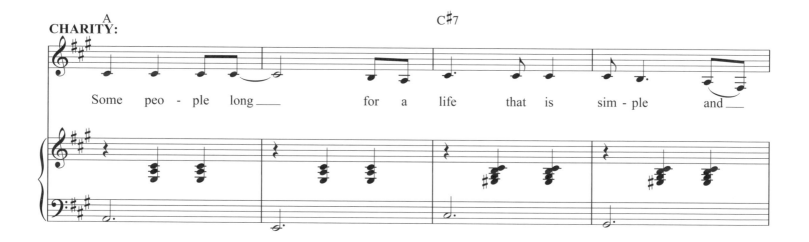

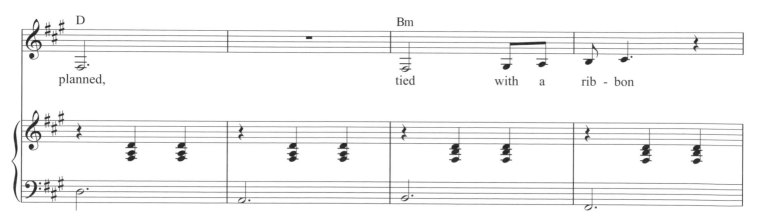

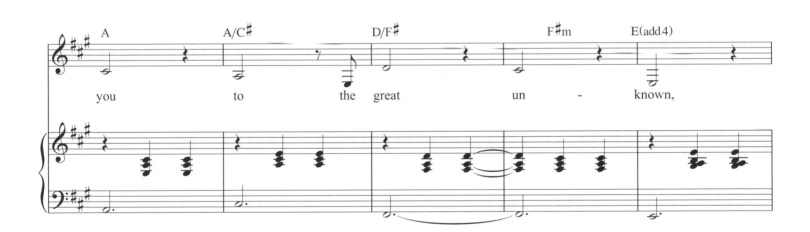

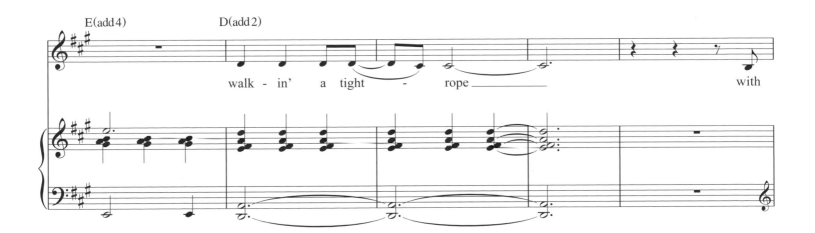

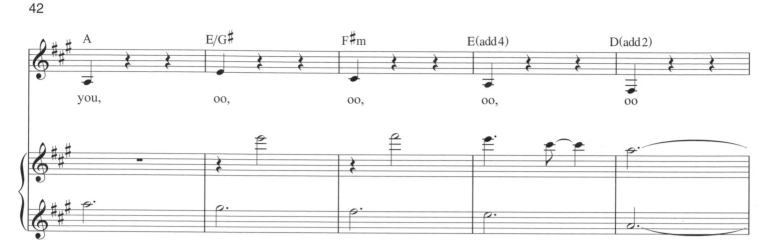

you, oo, oo, oo, oo

With you, oo,

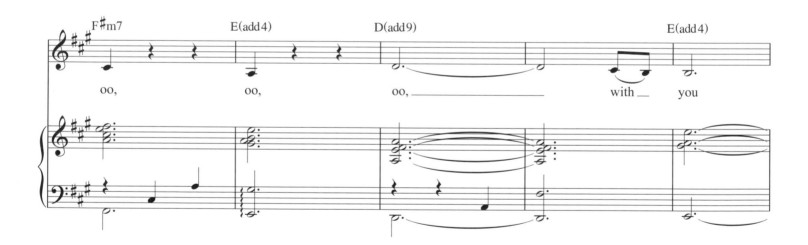

oo, oo, oo, _____ with __ you

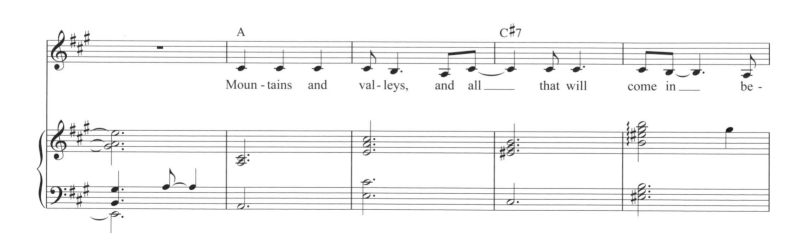

Moun-tains and val-leys, and all ___ that will come in ___ be-

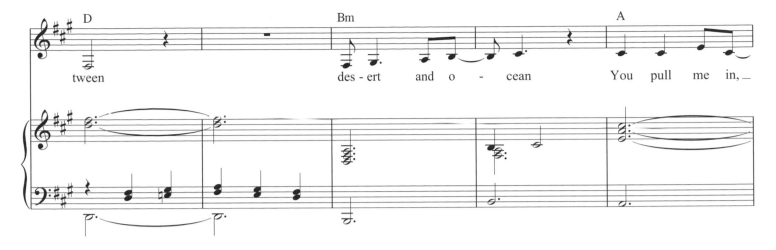

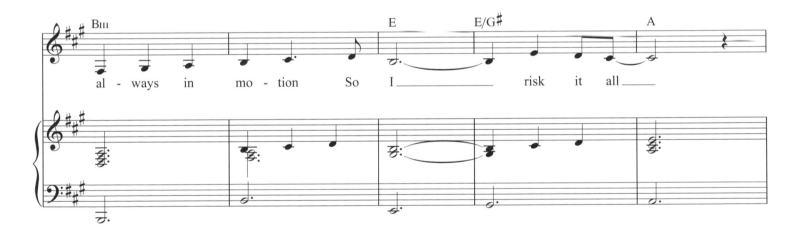

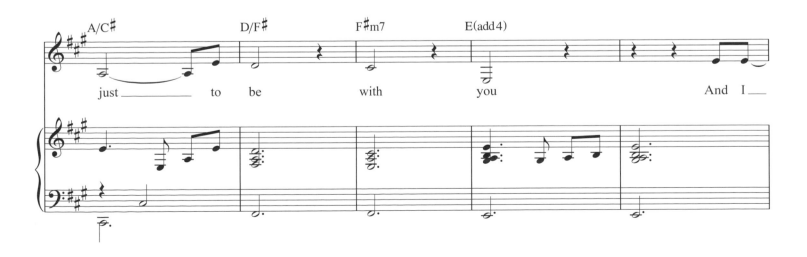

risk it all _____ for this life

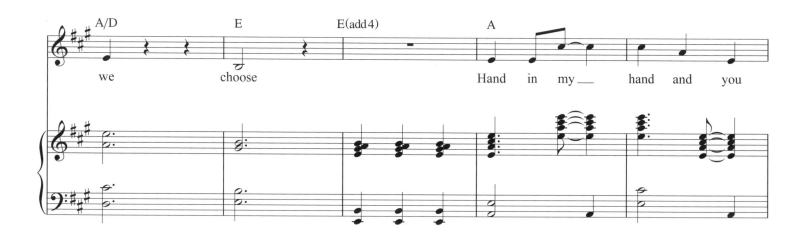

we choose Hand in my ___ hand and you

prom-ised to ___ nev-er let go We're walk-in' a tight-

-rope High in the sky, ___ we can see ___ the whole ___ world ___ down be-

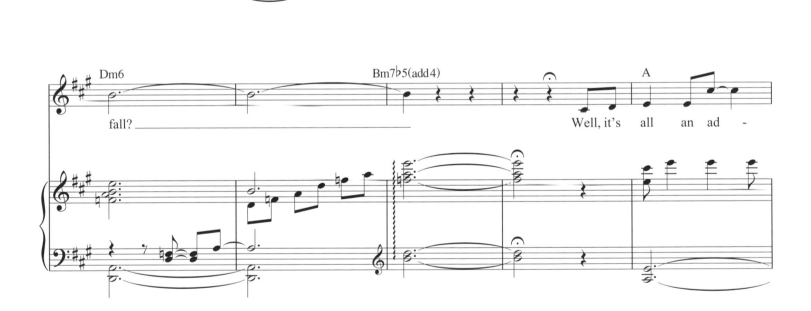

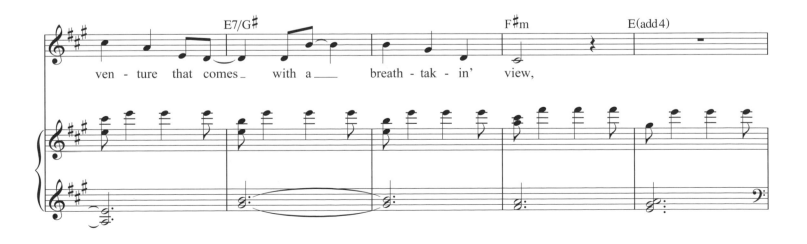

46

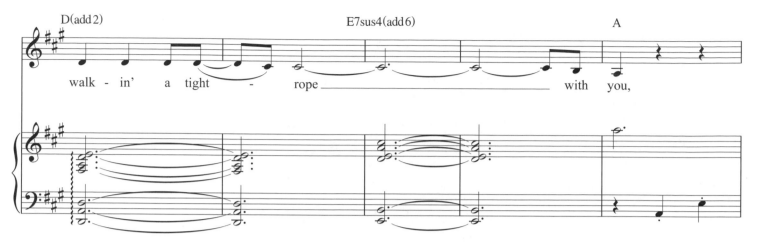

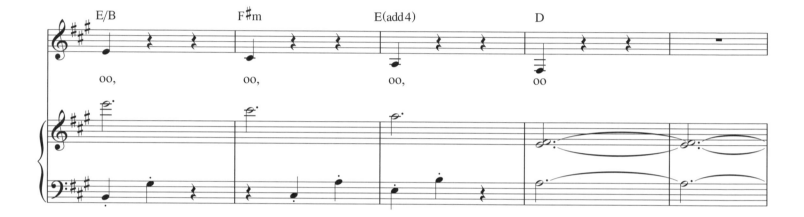

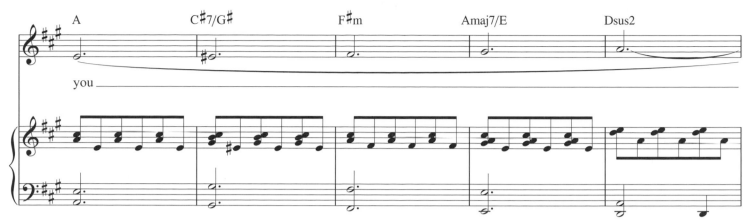

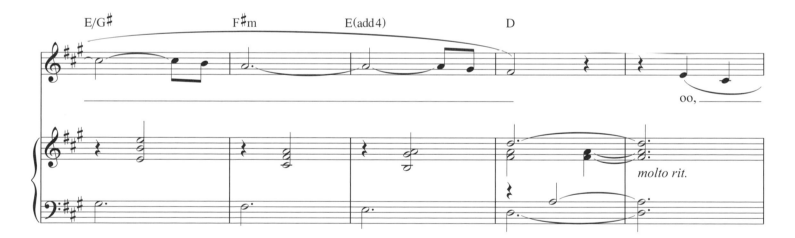

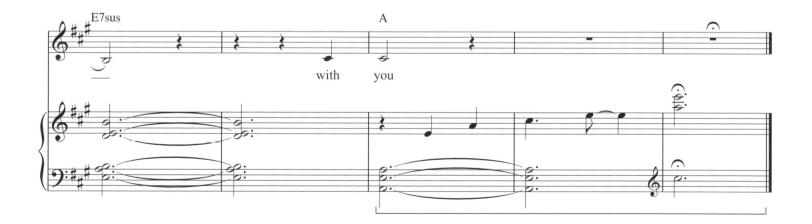

AUDITION
(The Fools Who Dream)
from *La La Land*

Music by Justin Hurwitz
Lyrics by Benj Pasek
& Justin Paul

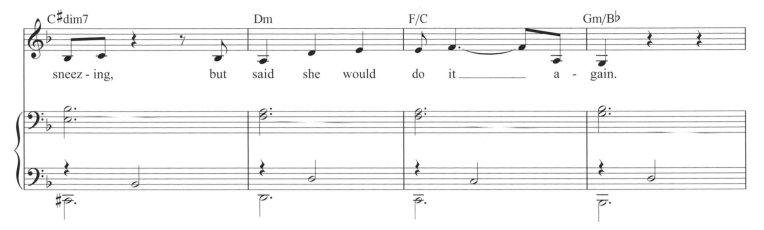

sneez - ing, but said she would do it _____ a - gain.

Here's to the ones who dream,

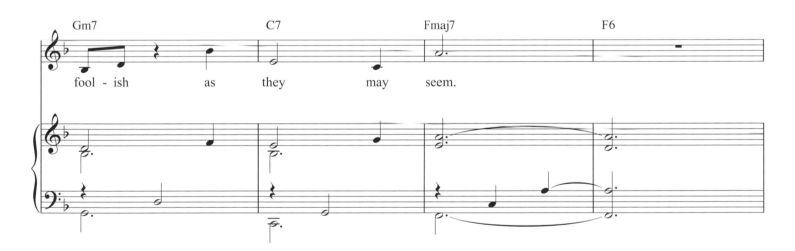

fool - ish as they may seem.

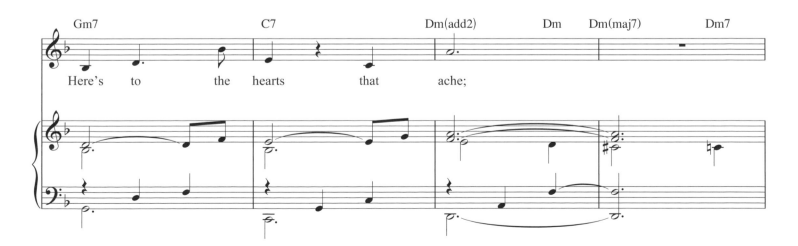

Here's to the hearts that ache;

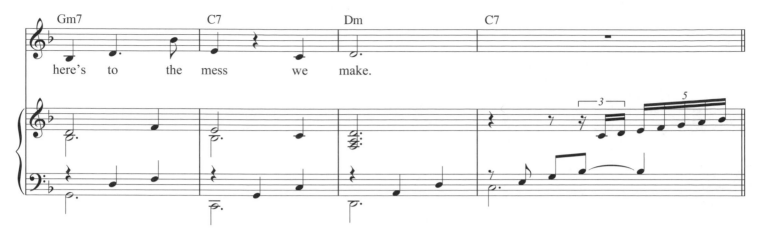

here's to the mess we make.

Faster

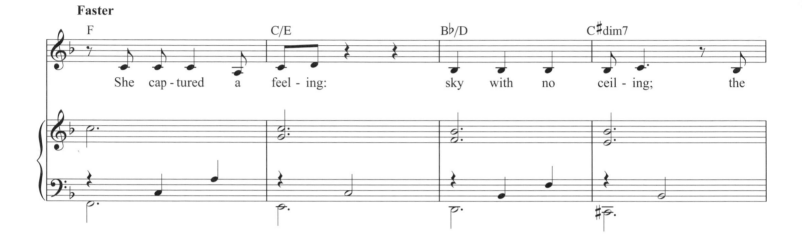

She cap-tured a feel-ing: sky with no ceil-ing; the

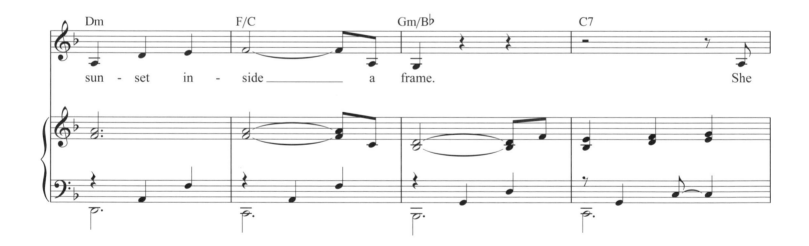

sun-set in-side a frame. She

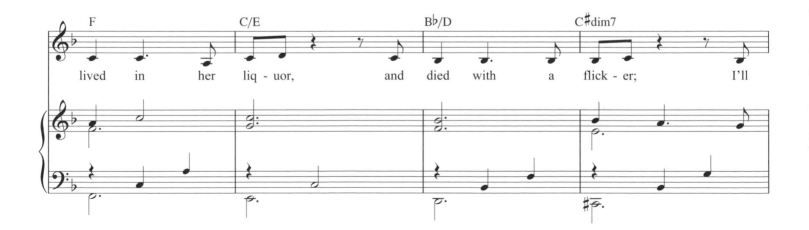

lived in her liq-uor, and died with a flick-er; I'll

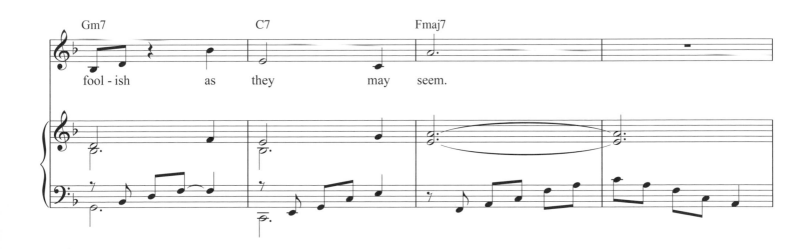

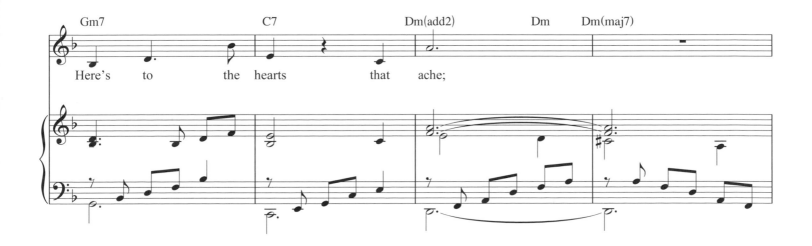

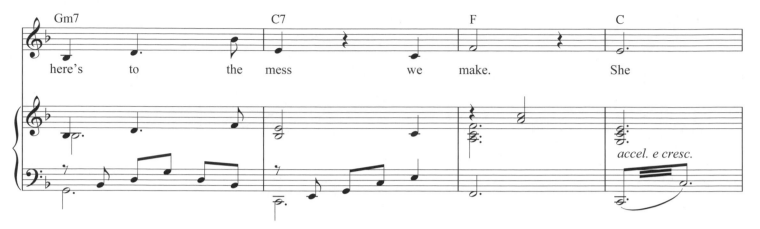

here's to the mess we make. She

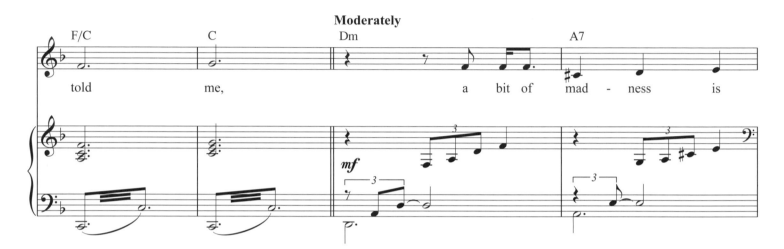

told me, a bit of mad - ness is

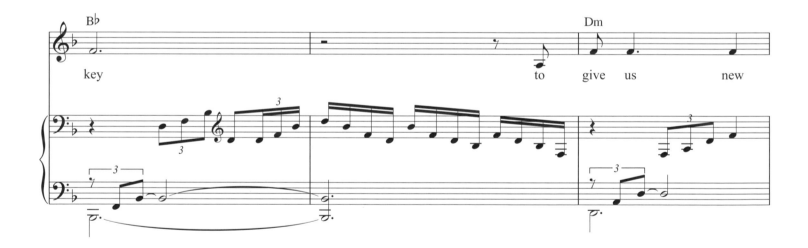

key to give us new

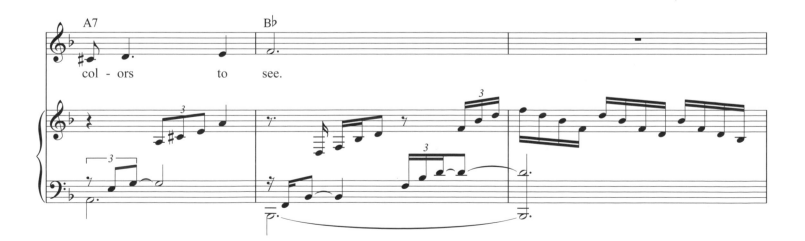

col - ors to see.

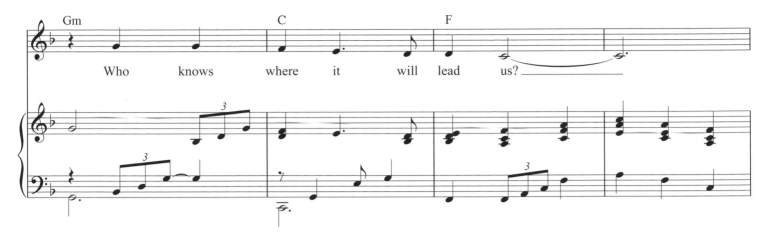

Who knows where it will lead us? _____

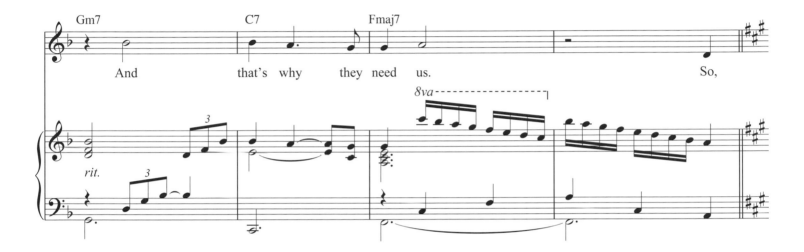

And that's why they need us. So,

Broadening

bring on _____ the reb - els, _____ the rip - ples from peb - bles, the

paint - ers and po - ets and ___ plays. And, _____

54

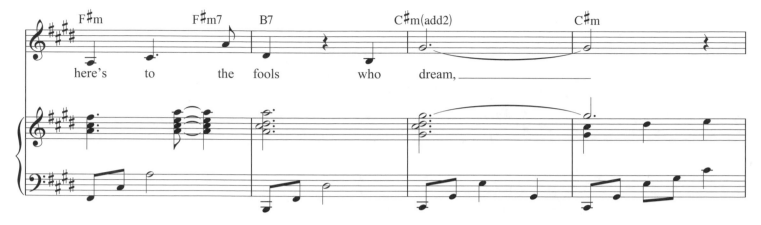

here's to the fools who dream,

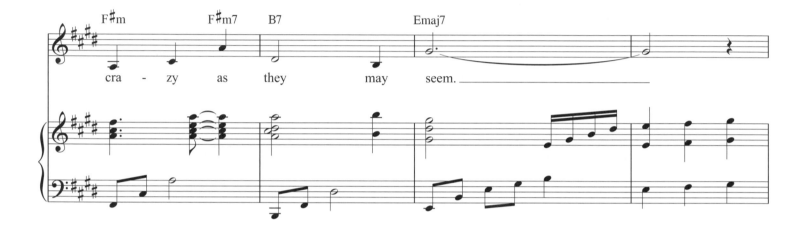

cra - zy as they may seem.

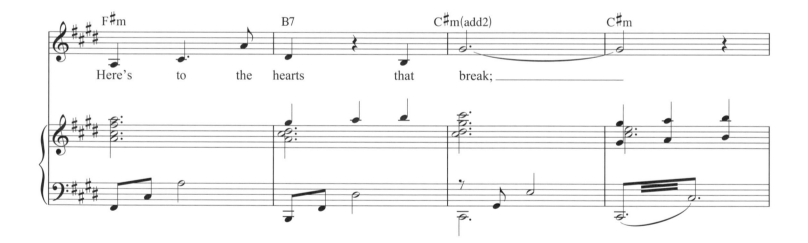

Here's to the hearts that break;

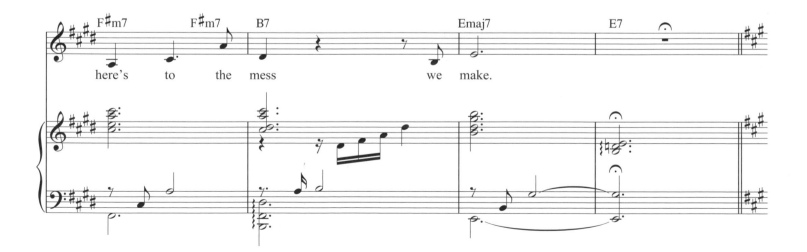

here's to the mess we make.

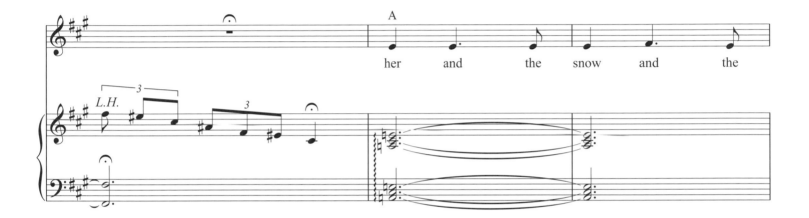

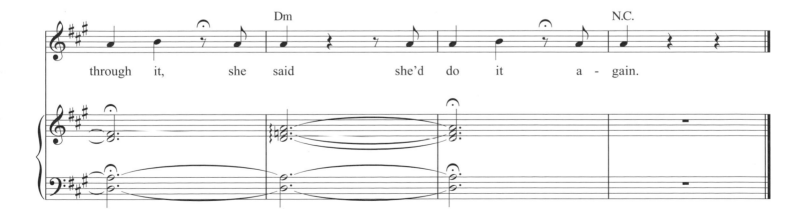

HOW FAR I'LL GO
from *Moana*

Music and Lyrics by
Lin-Manuel Miranda

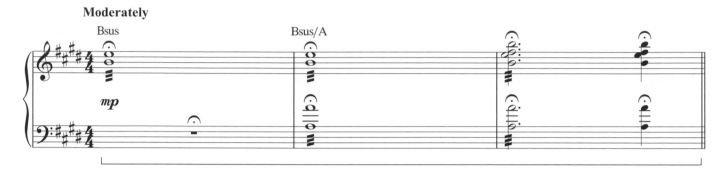

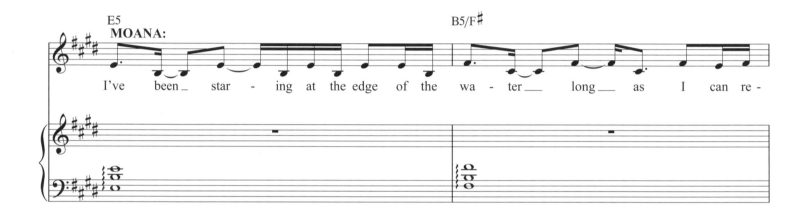

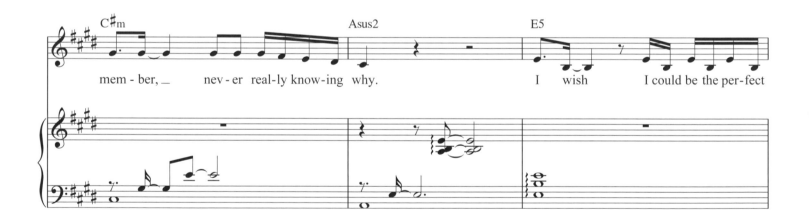

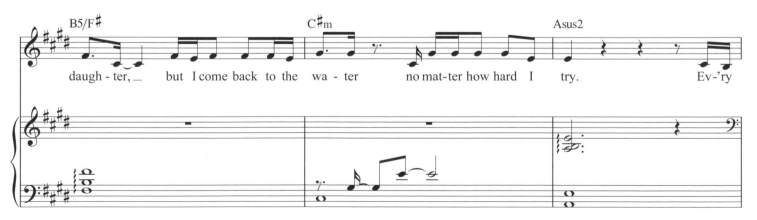

turn I take, ev-'ry trail I track, ev-'ry path I make, ev-'ry road leads back to the

place I know where I can-not go, where I long ___ to be. See the

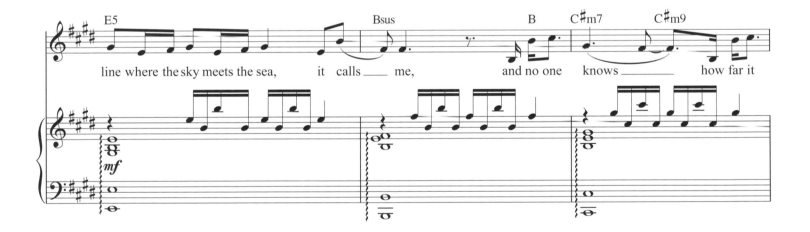

line where the sky meets the sea, it calls ___ me, and no one knows ___ how far it

goes. ___ If the wind in my sail on the sea stays be-hind ___ me, one day I'll

know. _____ If I go, there's just no tell-ing how far I'll go. I ____ know ___ ev-'ry-bod-y on this

is - land ___ seems ___ so hap-py on this is - land. ___ Ev-'ry-thing is by de - sign. ___

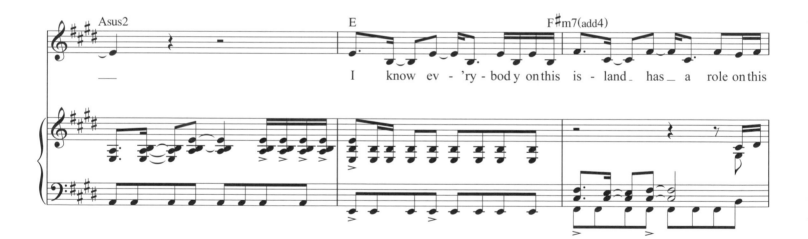

_____ I know ev-'ry-bod-y on this is - land ___ has ___ a role on this

is - land, ___ so may-be I can roll with mine. ___ I can

lead with pride, I can make us strong. I'll be sat-is-fied if I play a-long, but the

voice in-side sings a dif-f'rent song. What is wrong with me? See the

light as it shines on the sea: it's blind - ing, but no one knows _____ how deep it

goes. _____ And it seems like it's call-ing out to me, so come find ___ me and let me

know. _____ What's be - yond that line? Will I cross that line? The

line where the sky meets the sea, it calls __ me, _____ and no one knows _____ how far it

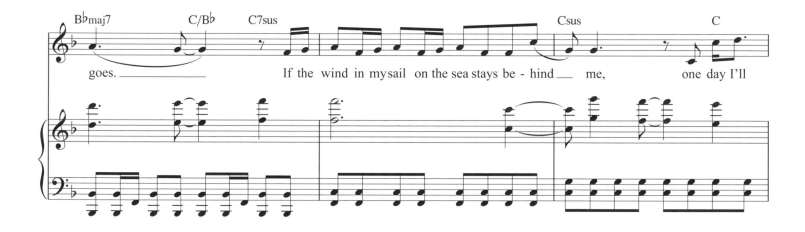

goes. _____ If the wind in my sail on the sea stays be - hind __ me, one day I'll

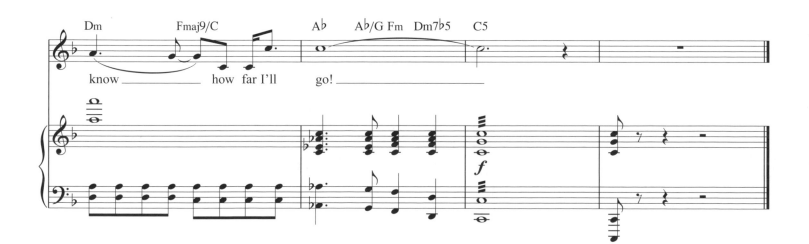

know _____ how far I'll go! _____

STILL HURTING

from *The Last Five Years*

Music and Lyrics by
Jason Robert Brown

62

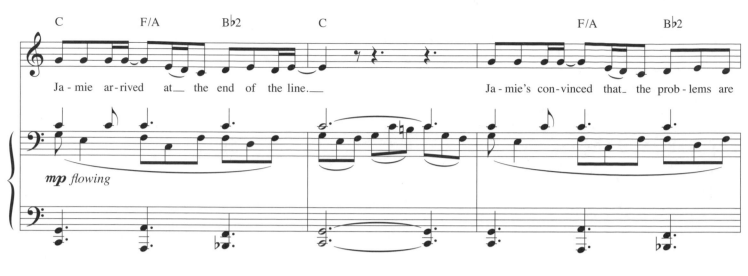

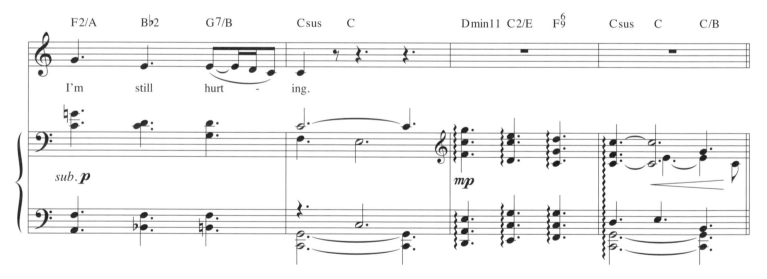

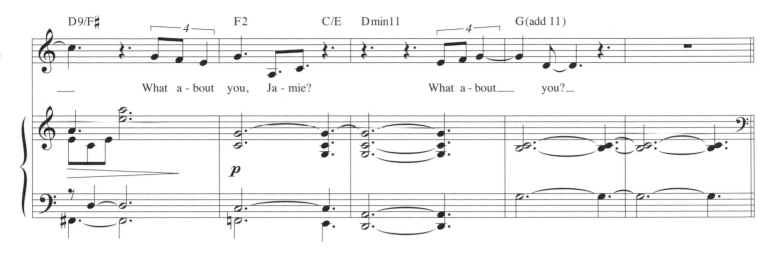

What a-bout you, Ja - mie? What a-bout____ you?____

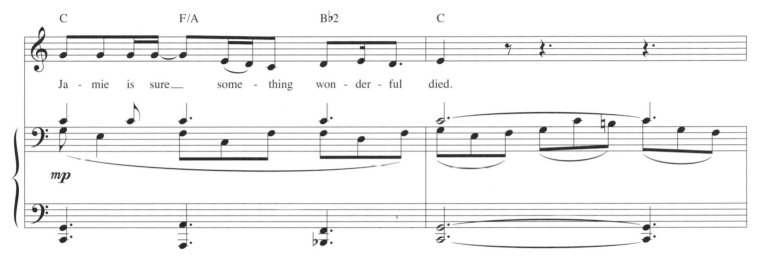

Ja - mie is sure____ some - thing won - der - ful died.

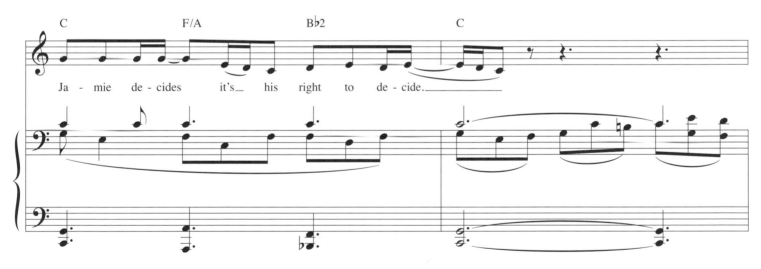

Ja - mie de - cides it's____ his right to de - cide.____

Ja - mie's got se - crets he does - n't con - fide,____ And

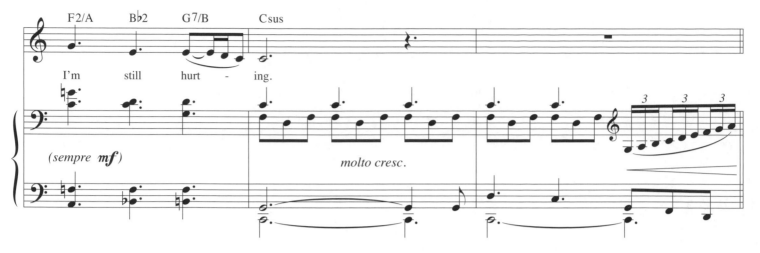

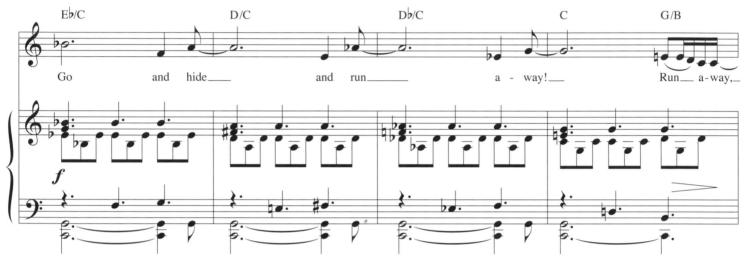

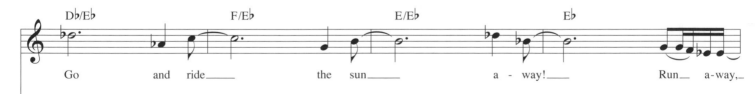

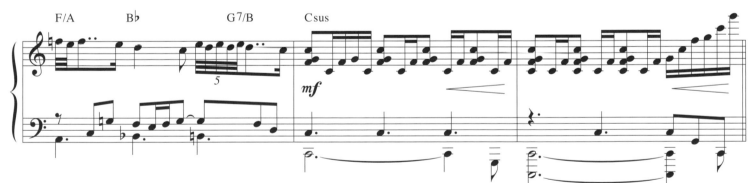

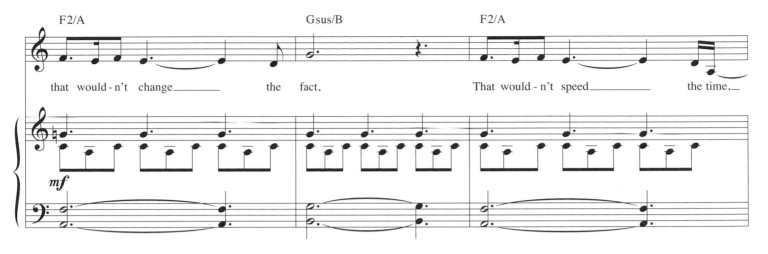

that would-n't change _____ the fact, That would-n't speed _____ the time,

Once the foun - da - tion's cracked And

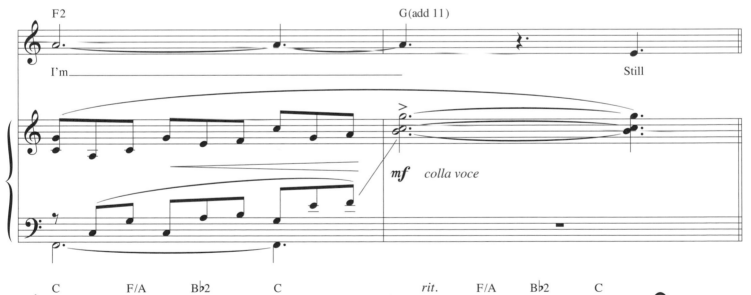

I'm _____ Still

hurt - ing.

WHEN WILL MY LIFE BEGIN?

from *Tangled*

Music by Alan Menken
Lyrics by Glenn Slater

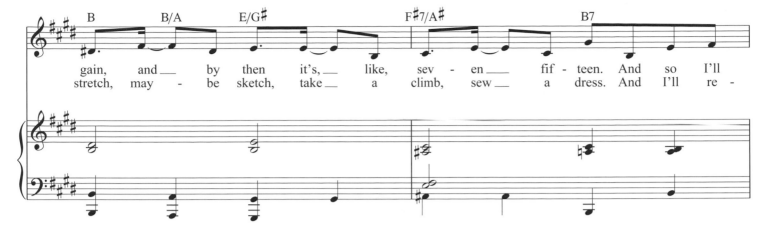

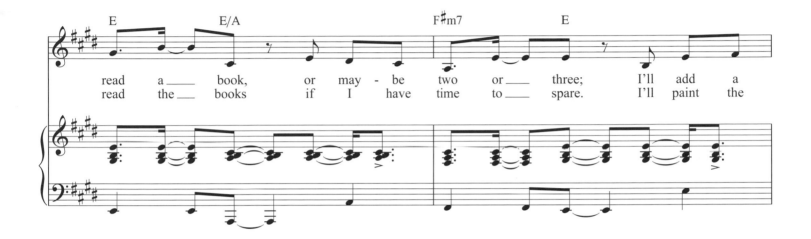

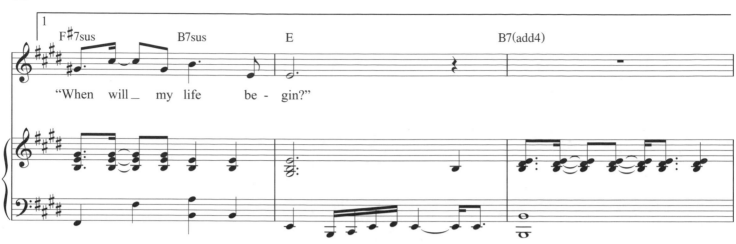

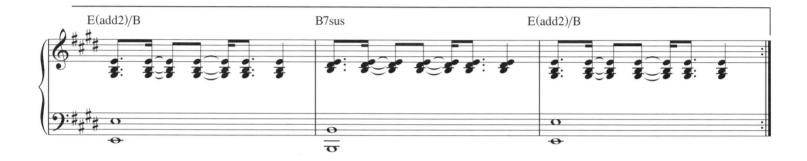

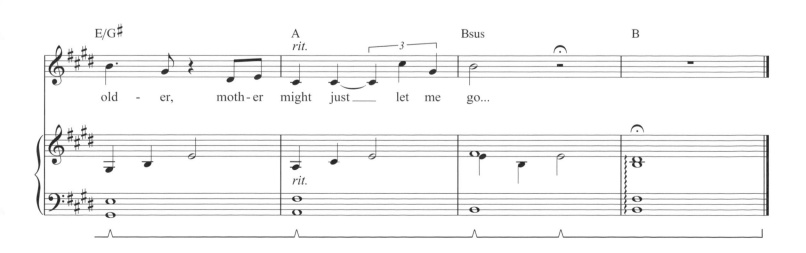